GAELIC GAMES
QUIZ BOOK
TYRONE

ALAN RODGERS

The
History
Press
Ireland

First published 2015

The History Press Ireland
50 City Quay
Dublin 2
Ireland

www.thehistorypress.ie

© Alan Rodgers, 2015

The right of Alan Rodgers to be identified as the Author
of this work has been asserted in accordance with the
Copyright, Designs and Patents Act 1988.

All rights reserved. No part of this book may be reprinted
or reproduced or utilised in any form or by any electronic,
mechanical or other means, now known or hereafter invented,
including photocopying and recording, or in any information
storage or retrieval system, without the permission in writing
from the Publishers.

British Library Cataloguing in Publication Data.
A catalogue record for this book is available from the British Library.

ISBN 978 1 84588 852 7

Typesetting and origination by The History Press

Contents

About the Compiler

This is the first venture for Alan Rodgers into a publication in the quiz genre, but as an author of some repute, he has mastered it.

A Tyrone-based journalist, Alan has written four books. Three of these, *Down from the Cross* (2006), *Forever Young on the Fields of Moy* (2008), and *Leading Through the Troubles* (2013), are GAA-based. The fourth, *Real Horses and Replicas*, is a local history publication that was described as a must-have book at its launch in 2011.

Introduction

So you really are a follower of Tyrone GAA and all its associated matters?

Good for you and congratulations on your good luck. For you are just about to read here the ultimate publication for a Tyrone GAA follower.

Yes, you have now got in your hands the *Gaelic Games Quiz Book: Tyrone* and it's jam-packed with all the questions you might ever have asked or wanted to ask about your favourite county.

This book has plenty more that you might ever have thought about in terms of GAA lore, since you don't have time to delve into the more obscure areas of results and achievements associated with the Red Hand county.

However, it's not always the so-called obscure questions that trip up the fan that knows everything about his or her club or county. Not by any means, since even the important facts and figures or dates and landmarks can slip away just when you're calling upon them.

So, if you are one of those fans who takes pride in coming up with little nuggets of information or if you just want to test yourself on Tyrone GAA for the sake of it – this quiz book is for you.

There are questions for everyone – some are simple and straightforward, some a bit more daunting and others will really test you out.

Hopefully, though, there is more than enough within these pages to keep you interested, amused, frustrated and puzzled – and to reinforce your enthusiasm for all things Tyrone.

Enjoy it!

Founder Members Make Their Mark

These were the people and events that led the way for the Tyrone GAA. The challenges they faced were immense, but their contributions laid the foundations for the strength of Gaelic games in the twenty-first century. But how much can you recall about those earliest years?

1. The first chairman of the GAA in Tyrone was a Strabane man, named Michael V. O'Nolan. One of his sons went on to achieve acclaim as a well-known writer under what names?

2. Tyrone's very first Ulster championship game took place against their new rivals from Armagh in January 1904. As well as being historic for this fact, the match also has another unusual claim to fame. What is it?

3. The Derrytresk club can rightly claim to be one of the oldest in the county and is proud of being the 'little club with the big heart.' An earlier club in the area was named after a Dutchman, H. Goff, who had come to the east Tyrone to do what?

4. One cup has the distinction of being the first to be played for in Tyrone. It was organised in the Mid-Tyrone area in 1906-07. Can you name the piece of silverware in question?

5. GAA history in Tyrone during the first decades of the twentieth century was dominated by collapse and revival. The first such revival took place in 1913-14 and the meeting was attended by which Ulster official who went on to become prominent in Irish life for other reasons?

6. Long periods without a championship win are now rare for Tyrone at senior inter-county level. However, it was to be 1926 before they eventually achieved a victory and the losses included one in 1920 to Armagh that was unique for what reason?

7. Tyrone's white jerseys with the Red Hand are famous. But before being introduced in the late 1920s, the county team played in a number of different colours. Their 1918 Ulster championship meeting against Monaghan saw them wear which colour?

8. A famous Tyrone poetess who died in 1891 was commemorated in the name of the very first camogie club to be established in the county. Can you name the club, which was based in Fintona?

9. In the modern era, Tyrone teams annually meet and beat the top teams in Ireland. It was all so different, though, a century ago. Name the year in which the county first lined out against the reigning All-Ireland champions.

10. Springfield Park in Dungannon was a regular venue for inter-county matches. Film footage of the 1929 Gold Medal meeting against Antrim is reckoned to be the oldest one of a Tyrone match. The game is also believed to be noteworthy for what other reason?

Unique Achievements

Achieving something which is truly ground-breaking is an honour shared by a few pioneers of the GAA in Tyrone. Their rare, and indeed unique, efforts towards the development of the Association in the Red Hand county spans over a century.

1. The area around Castlederg and Victoria Bridge in north Tyrone was the birthplace of one of the first vice-presidents of the GAA and another man who made an important contribution towards drawing up the rules of hurling. Can you name them?

2. George Sigerson, who was a native of Strabane, is well known for having donated the Sigerson Cup for inter-varsity football. The Strabane Sigersons GAA club is named after him. Can you name the popular Tyrone song that he composed?

3. A leading Tyrone man was chairman of the group that donated the Sam Maguire Cup as a prize for the All-Ireland senior football champions. Can you name him?

4. No Tyrone person has ever held the position of GAA president and only one native of the county is known to have stood for the position. This man let his name go forward in 1976 and was from the Moy club. Who is he?

5. Three men from the county have held the post of Ulster GAA President. Can you name them?

6. The post of 'Tyrone GAA president' was officially introduced in 2008 and has been held since then by a prominent former footballer with the Clonoe and Carrickmore clubs. Who is he?

7. Croke Park is one of the greatest sports stadiums in the world and it was designed by an architect who played as a Tyrone footballer in the 1960s. Who is he?

8. Tyrone GAA historian Joseph Martin also held an important post within the education sector. What was it?

9. Killyclogher's Brendan Harkin holds the distinction of being one of the youngest ever Tyrone chairmen. What age was he when he took the post in 1981?

10. Can you name the two natives of County Leitrim who have served as Tyrone County chairmen?

Who am I?

The 1930s and 1940s were an historic time for Tyrone as the county's teams began to make their mark at provincial and All-Ireland level. It was a time of enthusiasm and optimism and the personalities and players who made it all happen provide a test for your knowledge of this stirring period.

1. I won a county medal with my club, before representing my college at rugby. In 1942, I captained Tyrone to its first ever inter-county success in the Lagan Cup. Who am I?

2. In the 1920s and 1930s, I won county senior medals with a number of different clubs. I marked the great Larry Stanley in 1927 and represented Tyrone in the championship from 1923 until 1936. Who am I?

3. I was born in Charlemount and was associated with the Moy club. In 1928, I represented the United States in the Tailteann games. Who am I?

4. My club has gone on to become one of the strongest in Ulster and once won an All-Ireland club title. But I was on the first Tyrone team to win an Ulster minor title and scored a goal in an All-Ireland semi-final. Who am I?

5. I was one of three brothers on the Tyrone team. We played against Cavan in the 1933 Ulster final and met them again the following year. In that 1934 game, my goal would have given us a 2-5 to 2-4 win, but was disallowed by the referee. Who am I?

6. Injury ruled me out of the 1942 Lagan Cup final that Tyrone won, but that year was still a memorable one for my teammates and me in a big final at Croke Park. Who am I?

7. I was the first great goalkeeper from my club and there was nothing to worry about when I was in goal. I played for Tyrone in the 1933 Ulster final and lost three county finals with in a row with my club. Who am I?

8. Our team wasn't a Tyrone one, but our county still provided the backbone of players. In 1946, my team mate, Iggy Jones, scored one of the best goals ever seen in Croke Park and my tussle with Sean Purcell was another highlight. Who am I?

9. I made my debut as a substitute on the Tyrone team that won the Lagan Cup in 1942. However, although I represented the county in the Ulster championship until 1952, I'm better remembered as a former county secretary. Who am I?

10. I was on my club's first-ever O'Neill Cup-winning team and represented Tyrone in the championship in the 1940s. But my nephew was more successful as a player and manager with his county, Donegal. Who am I?

Round

4

Men on the Line who Made the Decisions

Mickey Harte has been in charge of Tyrone teams since the early 1990s. But he's not the first to enjoy success at inter-county level and the managers – or men on the line who made the decisions – are still fondly remembered for their roles in historic triumphs for the O'Neill county.

1. Who was the County Down man who played an integral part in coaching the 1956 and 1957 Ulster title-winning sides?

2. When Tyrone won the Ulster senior title in 1973, Jody O'Neill was the manager. He continued to manage the seniors until what year?

3. Which two men – one a member of the 1956 and 1957 Tyrone teams – were in charge of the minors when they reached the All-Ireland final in 1972 and won it in 1973?

4. Art McRory's first stint as Tyrone senior manager began in 1980. But who did he replace in the post that year?

5. Harry Brennan, from Castlederg, was involved with the Tyrone minor teams when they won the Ulster title. In what year was this?

6. Who managed the Tyrone minor team that won the Ulster title in 1988?

7. How many provincial finals did Tyrone minors appear in under the management of Mickey Harte?

8. Liam Donnelly of Trillick and Martin Coyle of Ardboe managed the county minors to All-Ireland titles in 2001 and 2004. Who succeeded them in the role?

9. Can you name the two assistants to Mickey Harte when he guided Tyrone to their first All-Ireland senior title in 2003?

10. Which manager guided Tyrone to their first ever National League final in 1992?

Top Aces in Handball

Asmall core of clubs have led the way on the handball courts of Ulster, Ireland and the world. The game is currently enjoying a golden period of progress with players winning titles at all levels. There have been many noteworthy moments at 40x20 and 60x30, and this round provides an insight into some of the most significant.

1. In 1970, a Tyrone player made history by becoming the first from the county to win an All-Ireland Handball title. His club was Loughmacrory and he captured the 40x20 junior softball crown. Can you name him?

2. Handball has a long history in the mid-Tyrone area, but in 1910 a grand challenge game was played between Pomeroy and players from what other Tyrone village not usually renowned for its prowess in the sport?

3. 2014 was a particularly special year for Tyrone handball, with players winning the All-Ireland U-16 and minor titles among many others. The first ever All-Ireland underage title was won by Ciaran Curran in what year and what age group?

4. Which member of the historic Tyrone senior football team which won their first Ulster title in 1956 went on to become a leading handball official and player in subsequent years?

5. A number of the new-style 40x20 handball alleys were first erected in Tyrone during the 1970s. The locations included Beragh, Loughmacrory, Pomeroy and Carrickmore. Which club not among this list holds the distinction of building the first?

6. Ciaran Curran ranks as the only Tyrone player ever to have reached an All-Ireland senior final. He was defeated in that decider by Michael 'Duxie' Walsh of Kilkenny. What was special about that final?

7. Three players from the Red Hand county have won All-Ireland minor titles. The latest success was recorded in 2014. Can you name the player and his club?

8. The trophy for the Tyrone senior handball championship is named after which former stalwart of the sport in the county?

9. In what year was the first recorded handball alley in Loughmacrory believed to have been built?

10. What new facility was opened in Loughmacrory in 2014?

With the Referees

There would, of course, be no games without the referees. Their abilities are often questioned in the heat of competitive matches, but there's no doubting their commitment or dedication. Many from Tyrone have also made their mark at the highest level.

1. Paddy Devlin is the only referee from a Tyrone club to have ever taken charge of All-Ireland senior football finals. Can you name the years and his native county?

2. In 1982, Jack Heaney took charge of the All-Ireland minor final between Dublin and Kerry. Can you name the appropriately titled public house that he still runs in Sixmilecross?

3. The first man to referee three Tyrone finals in a row (from 1943 to 1945) was Paddy Gallagher from Omagh. He later died while refereeing a final in which Ulster competition?

4. Can you name the last Tyrone referee and his club to take charge of an All-Ireland U-21 football final?

5. In the past half-century there has been just one referee of a Tyrone senior county final from outside the county. Can you name him and his club and county?

6. Why does the 2011 Tyrone senior final, which was won by Clonoe, hold a unique place in the recent history of the county's showpiece occasion?

7. When Tyrone reached the 1986 All-Ireland final, many within the county could have been slightly perturbed by the referee. But for what reason?

8. For many years, Jack Martin was a prominent referee from Omagh's St Enda's club. He also holds a specific record for a Tyrone referee at All-Ireland level. What is it?

9. A well-known Tyrone hurling referee also holds a special achievement at the top level of inter-county hurling. What is it?

10. Jim Curran received recognition at national level as a referee by being given charge of which two major finals?

Which Club am I?

Our clubs are the backbone of the GAA in the county. Their leaps of faith in the earliest days of the Association made a decisive difference and they continue to play a vital role within their communities. We all know about our own areas, so this round is a little test on our knowledge of other clubs.

1. We are based in north Tyrone and our club was formed as a result of an amalgamation in 1970. A highlight for us was reaching the senior football final and winning a senior hurling title. Which club are we?

2. It was in 1965 that our club was re-formed, but the roots of the GAA locally go back to the start of the twentieth century. Our sole O'Neill Cup success came in the twenty-first century and during an historic year for Tyrone. Which club are we?

3. Our base is on the shores of Lough Neagh and one of our county finals was once played in December. The last time we won the O'Neill Cup was in the 1990s and our new pitch development is at Aneeter. Which club are we?

4. Our club was formed by a man from Kerry, but our colours are the same as a famous hurling county. We won eight senior championships in a row and are currently in the process of developing a new pitch. Which club are we?

5. In 2003, our ground was named as the best maintained and presented venue in Ulster. We won junior and intermediate titles in the space of four seasons and reached a senior final in the fifth. Our camogie team was the first in Tyrone. Which club are we?

6. Our club is named after one of the leaders of the 1916 Easter Rising. Both of our county final appearances resulted in defeats. Which club are we?

7. St Mary's Park is our home ground and we hold a record in Tyrone football as a team which once won promotion to senior ranks in rather unusual circumstances. We are past junior and intermediate champions and our club name is also St Mary's. Which club are we?

8. Like the Mayo footballers, it was once said that our quest for a senior football title was jinxed and there was a time when we played in competitions outside Tyrone. But we have now won three O'Neill Cups. Which club are we?

9. Many of our players won senior championship medals in the past and our club was the first from Tyrone to win an Ulster intermediate title. We have also reached a provincial junior final and we had a player on the 1986 Tyrone team. Which club are we?

10. The first club in our parish was formed in 1906 and we hold two unique records in Tyrone football. Our ground was the first in Tyrone to have a covered stand and the trophy for the county's senior ladies championship is named after one of our former members. Which club are we?

Round
8

Hurlers on the Ditch

The hurlers were the only Tyrone county team to play in Croke Park in 2014. Their Nickey Rackard Cup success was historic and it's not the first remarkable achievement by the hurlers. This round highlights some of the others.

1. What was the impressive achievement of Dungannon and Tyrone hurler Eamon Devlin during the county's 1994 National League campaign?

2. In 1973, Gerry Goodwin played for the Tyrone minors when they won the All-Ireland title. Do you know what his other notable and unique distinction is for someone from the county?

3. It is well known that Peter Canavan was once a member of Killyclogher hurling club. But one of his attacking colleagues on the starting team for the 1995 All-Ireland football final had a more notable hurling distinction. Who was he and what was his achievement?

4. When Tyrone won the All-Ireland junior title in 1996, the team included many dual players. Only one of them, however, also represented the county in the Ulster senior football championship. Who was he?

5. Tyrone have won two Lory Meagher and one Nicky Rackard title since the competitions were introduced in 2005. But which three teams have they defeated in the final at Croke Park?

6. It would take some effort to calculate the number of Croke Park appearances for Tyrone club and county football teams. Can you provide the corresponding figure for hurling teams from the county?

7. Can you name the captain of the Tyrone hurling team that in 2014 won the Nicky Rackard Cup title for the first time?

8. Vinny Owens, who captained Tyrone to their All-Ireland junior hurling title in 1996, is the only hurler from the county to do what?

9. Armagh native Mattie Lennon was the manager of the Tyrone hurling team which won the 2014 Nicky Rackard Cup. But can you name the manager whom he succeeded and his native county?

10. In recent years, the Tyrone hurlers have played in the Ulster senior hurling championship. Can you name the last year in which they did so and the team that defeated them in the first round at Omagh?

Camogie to the Fore

The game of camogie was created in the early twentieth century and has enjoyed a vibrant history within Tyrone. The first teams competed between 1910 and 1920, and the girls have continued to overcome many challenges and prosper during the subsequent decades as well.

1. Tyrone camogie enjoyed its first great growth spurt in the 1930s. Among the special achievements was one by the then county secretary and county captain, Vera Campbell. What was it?

2. Eglish are, and have been, the dominant force in Tyrone camogie since their formation in 1965. How many county titles have they won during that period?

3. A team from the Red Hand county has played at Croke Park on one occasion in its history. Can you name the year and the competition?

4. Since the formation of the Eglish camogie club in 1965, they have dominated the Tyrone senior title. Which sides that have broken their stranglehold?

5. Ann Jordan, Urusla Jordan and Maureen Ogle (Eglish), Teresa Kelly (Carrickmore) and Josephine McLaughlin (Dungannon) made history by achieving what honour in 1979?

6. Which former Tyrone GAA chairman currently serves in the same post on the county's camogie board?

7. Recent years have seen a revival of camogie in a number of clubs. Which two teams, also renowned for their hurling prowess, contested the 2011 and 2013 junior finals?

8. Eglish hold the distinction of being the only Tyrone team to have reached an All-Ireland club final. Can you name the years in which they progressed to the final?

9. In 2014, the Tyrone camogie team won the Ulster intermediate title by defeating Cavan in the final. Who was the player of the match in that game?

10. The All-Ireland Camogie Féile Na nGael competition was held in Tyrone and Ulster in 2014. Which Tyrone clubs took part in the competition?

The New Kids on the Block from Ladies Football

Ladies football matches were played as part of sports days in the 1970s in some parts of Tyrone and it was in the 1990s that the youngest sport in the GAA family was first properly developed. Since then the progress has been immense and the achievements memorable!

1. When Tyrone reached and won the All-Ireland junior final in 1999, the presentation afterwards in the old Hogan Stand was notable. Why was this the case and who was the team captain?

2. The Tyrone ladies team reached their first All-Ireland senior final in 2010. Can you name the team captain and her club and the names of the management duo in that historic season?

3. 2000 was an important year for Tyrone, when they won the Ulster title and reached the National League final. Which four players received All Star awards that year in recognition of their outstanding play?

4. The Jarleth Kerr Cup is presented to the winners of the Tyrone senior ladies championship. Which trophy did it replace?

5. Eilish Gormley was one of the key players for Tyrone over many years. In the 1999 All-Ireland junior final her scoring exploits were especially noteworthy. How much did she score?

6. On how many occasions have the Tyrone minor ladies reached the All-Ireland final?

7. Carrickmore and St Macartan's have dominated the Tyrone ladies senior championship. Two clubs from the county have also won the Ulster title; Carrickmore are one, who are the second?

8. In 2007, Greencastle became the first team from Tyrone to win an All-Ireland club title. Their ladies, Sperrin Óg, followed that success up by winning the junior ladies All-Ireland in what year?

9. How many Ulster senior titles in ladies football have been won by Tyrone, and in what year did they last claim the title?

10. Gemma Begley remains one of the Tyrone's most prolific scorers in ladies football. She claimed a first for the county in 2014 during the inter-provincial series that was won by Ulster. What was it?

Schooldays were the Best of our Lives

No Tyrone team has been more successful than the Vocational Schools side. Add in the many triumphs enjoyed by individual schools and there's every reason to believe that those were the best of days for many footballers who went on to greater things in the future.

1. Which former Fermanagh county star – along with future senior manager Art McRory – helped organise and train the first Tyrone Vocational Schools team to win an All-Ireland?

2. That 1967 team was just the third from the county to win an All-Ireland at Croke Park. It was captained by which player, whose son has enjoyed many similar triumphs at the venue?

3. Peter Canavan played at corner forward for the Tyrone team that won the All-Ireland Vocational Schools title in 1988. Why might the 1989 success for them at Croke Park also be classed as memorable for him?

4. Which member of the 1973 Tyrone minor team went on, in 1974, to captain Omagh CBS to their first MacRory Cup title and represent the county seniors for the first time in the Ulster championship?

5. Tyrone achieved a schools first in 1997 by winning the double of All-Ireland Vocational Schools and Hogan Cup titles. Who were the two winning captains?

6. Joe McMahon and Dermot Carlin were two future All-Ireland senior winners on the 2001 Omagh CBS team that won the MacRory Cup title. But what was unusual about their success?

7. Can you name the three members of the starting team that represented Omagh CBS when they won the Hogan Cup for the first time in 2007 and who were inter-county senior footballers in 2014?

8. The 2009 MacRory Cup final was the last year in which the competition was won by a Tyrone school. As well as having that unwelcome distinction, what notable first for the competition does it also have?

9. Tyrone have been a dominant force on the inter-county Vocational Schools scene since the 1960s. Can you name the first and last years of their All-Ireland titles?

10. 1997 was the first year in which Tyrone teams completed the Hogan Cup and All-Ireland Vocational Schools double. It's only been done twice by the county. What was the second year?

Round 12

County Senior Finals

For over 100 years, the county senior final has been the highlight of the club GAA year in the O'Neill county. The stories and events of those matches have provided many historic moments that continue to hold a special place in the history of the teams involved.

1. Carrickmore was the third club to win three O'Neill Cup titles in a row. Can you name the teams that they defeated in the finals between 1977 and 1979?

2. What was especially noteworthy about the first ever success for Derrylaughan in the O'Neill Cup in 1967?

3. Patience finally paid dividends for Dromore when they won the county senior title for the first time in 2007. How many finals had they lost prior to that big breakthrough?

4. Clonoe's second of three-in-a-row county titles came at the end of the 1950s. For what reason was their final pairing against Omagh in the 1959 decider unique?

5. The rivalry between Carrickmore and Errigal Ciaran has gone on for many decades. How many county senior finals have they contested, including replays, since 1991?

6. How many different clubs succeeded in winning the O'Neill Cup in the years between 2000 and 2014?

7. Strabane's last Tyrone senior title came when they defeated Dungannon in the 1945 final. But that decider at Omagh also holds another special distinction. What is it?

8. How many clubs have achieved the honour of winning a three-in-a-row of Tyrone senior titles?

9. The last drawn Tyrone senior final was between Errigal Ciaran and Carrickmore in 2006. How many of the finals played since the first in 1904 have finished level? Is it six, eight or nine?

10. The Tyrone senior championship has been organised since 1904, but was not played on a number of occasions. In what year, then, will the centenary of the competition take place?

Round

13

Do You Remember that County Final?

E ach county final provides GAA fans with special memories and each of them have produced their own specific niche. But how much is remembered about those games and the stories behind the headline victories?

1. Healy Park in Omagh is now the accepted venue for all county senior finals. In what year did the last final take place outside that venue and where was it held?

2. The 1991 final was a local derby between Coalisland and Clonoe. For what other reason was that final worthy of note?

3. Can you name the common denominator that links the Tyrone senior finals of 1904/05, 1927, 1934, 1937, 1973 and 1995?

4. The ten-year period between 1967 and 1977 was notable for new teams winning the Tyrone senior title. Can you name the clubs that achieved their big breakthroughs in that period?

5. Dungannon Clarkes led the Tyrone SFC roll of honour both before and after their tenth title-success in 1956. But in what year were they finally overtaken as the club with the most O'Neill Cup triumphs?

6. Can you name the two first-time finalists defeated in the 1975 and 1985 county finals? Both have not reached the final again.

7. The turnaround between the 1950 and 1951 finals was the most spectacular of all. Moortown won the title by defeating Dungannon in 1950, but their defeat the following year ranks as the heaviest ever in a county final. How many points did they lose by?

8. The Patsy Forbes Trophy for the top scorer in the Tyrone senior championship was once sponsored by Plunkett McCusker Trophies. Tommy Fiddis won the award for the first time. In what year was this award first made?

9. Which is the only club to have finished a county final scoreless, their final opponents on that occasion and the year of the decider?

10. The first county final replay was in 1907-08 and there have been eight during the intervening period. In what year was the last final drawn?

Testing your Memory on this Century's O'Neill Cup Deciders

Time passes quickly and the turn of the century seems like it was only yesterday. All of the county finals since 2000 have been played at Healy Park in Omagh and they have produced notable achievements for a host of different clubs and players. Here's a test on how much you remember.

1. There have been fourteen Tyrone senior finals since the start of this century. How many of those deciders have finished level?

2. Which former club stars were honoured during the half-time break at the 2000 county final?

3. Can you name the manager and captain of the Killyclogher team that won the Paddy O'Neill Cup for the first time in 2003?

4. Four of the teams that have captured the senior title during that time have been managed by people who are not natives of Tyrone. Can you name the quartet?

5. Can you name the other quartet of successful O'Neill Cup-winning managers this century who were also members of the clubs they guided to the title?

6. Just two players have the honour of having won Tyrone senior medals and All-Ireland senior medals in the one year. Who are they?

7. Carrickmore is the most productive team this century in terms of the number of finals reached. How many deciders have they reached during that time?

8. The 2009 final saw Dromore take the O'Neill Cup for a second time. The win over Dromore was especially memorable for two reasons for Colm McCullagh. What were they?

9. When Omagh St Enda's lost the 2005 final, what had been particularly noteworthy about their path to the decider that might have left them just a little bit tired?

10. Of the clubs which have reigned supreme in the Tyrone championship since 2000, which of them have proved to be most successful in terms of winning the O'Neill Cup?

On the
Ulster Club Front

In the modern era, the provincial club championships have become an added and increasingly important focus for Tyrone's top club teams. Each year they have moved onto the Ulster club stage with confidence and hope.

1. Errigal Ciaran are the only Tyrone team to win the Ulster club senior title. Can you name the two clubs they defeated in those provincial deciders in 1992 and 2002?

2. Which four other Tyrone clubs that have progressed to Ulster club senior finals and the years?

3. Apart from Errigal Ciaran, which clubs from Tyrone have played in the most Ulster club matches?

4. Carrickmore top the Tyrone roll of honour, but in what year did they enjoy their most successful Ulster club campaign?

5. How many games did Errigal Ciaran require to defeat Crossmaglen in the first round of the Ulster Club in 2002 and who did they subsequently defeat in the final to win the title?

6. In the 2004 championship, which teams did Carrickmore defeat to reach the semi-finals where they lost to St Gall's?

7. For what reason was the very first appearance by a Tyrone team in the Ulster club championship in 1968 unique?

8. The meeting of Errigal Ciaran and Ballinderry in the 2012 Ulster club was unusual for what fact?

9. Clonoe have appeared in the Ulster club championship on four occasions. Can you name the teams that defeated them at the first hurdle in 2008 and 2013?

10. Only once in the history of the provincial senior championship has a club been nominated to represent Tyrone. Can you name the club in question and the year?

The Ulster Junior and Intermediate Scenes

The Ulster club senior championship has been a feature of the GAA scene since the 1960s. In the past decade, the intermediate and junior provincial championships have also grown, and the All-Ireland finals in Croke Park prove a massive incentive. How have Tyrone teams fared?

1. In what year were Tyrone teams first represented in the official Ulster intermediate and junior club championships?

2. Which Tyrone clubs have emerged as the Ulster intermediate champions and the years of their successes?

3. Four clubs have won the Ulster club junior title. Can you name them and the years that they emerged as champions?

4. In 2005, the very first All-Ireland junior and intermediate finals were special for two reasons. One was that they were played in Portlaoise. But what was the other?

5. Who were the captain and manager of the Greencastle team that won the All-Ireland junior crown in 2007?

6. Greencastle and Cookstown have both won All-Ireland titles. But which Tyrone clubs teams also reached All-Ireland finals, but then lost?

7. Can you name the only Tyrone hurling team to have reached an All-Ireland club final and the year?

8. Which players from Tyrone have lined out in both an All-Ireland Club intermediate or junior football final and an All-Ireland senior football inter-county decider?

9. Which Tyrone clubs have progressed to but then lost Ulster intermediate or junior finals?

10. Owen Mulligan's success in winning two All-Ireland club titles with Cookstown brought him a unique distinction within the annals of the Tyrone GAA. What is it?

The All-County Leagues

The traditional 2.15 p.m. and 3.45 p.m. starts to All-County League games on a Sunday afternoon ensured a regularity that increased the popularity of club games in the 1970s and 1980s. The starred matches and mid-week fixtures have brought change, while the quest for titles remains as intense as ever.

1. What format of competition at club level preceded the introduction of the All-County Leagues for Tyrone in 1969?

2. In what year was the three-division system officially adopted for the Tyrone leagues?

3. Carrickmore's success in winning the 2013 senior league title extended their lead at the top of the roll of honour. But what was particularly significant about their win?

4. Between 1974 and 1986, Trillick won five O'Neill Cup titles. How many senior league crowns did they win in the period from 1973 until 1987?

5. Clonoe O'Rahilly's won the 2012 league title by defeating their neighbours and rivals from Coalisland. Was that triumph their first or second Division One success?

6. Since the turn of the century and up until 2014, how many all-county League Division One titles have been won by Dromore?

7. What was the major – and short-lived – change introduced for the All-County Leagues for the 1999 season?

8. In the period between 2000 and 2013, how many clubs completed the senior championship and All-County League Division One double?

9. Peter Canavan managed Errigal Ciaran to the Division One league title in 2010. But how many league titles did he win with the club as a player?

10. Which clubs were promoted from Divisions Two and Three at the end of the 2013 season?

Those History-Making Tyrone Minors

P resent-day GAA fans are accustomed to regular All-Ireland titles coming to Tyrone. It's a situation far removed from the mid-1940s when the national breakthrough arrived in great style and ensured that the players and teams involved carved a special niche for themselves in the annals.

1. Omagh's Dan McCaffrey was a key member of the Tyrone minor team that won the All-Ireland for the first time in 1947. But which club in the league of Ireland did he go on to star for in the 1950s?

2. The 1947 minors were the first team representing the county to play in Croke Park. Who holds the distinction of being the very first Tyrone player to score there?

3. A future president of the GAA lined out for the Mayo team beaten by Tyrone in that All-Ireland final. Can you name him?

4. Following Tyrone's victory in the 1947 Ulster minor final, it was decided to enlist the help of a trainer for the All-Ireland campaign. Who was he?

5. Which five members of the 1947 Tyrone minor team were also part of the team that claimed the title again in 1948?

6. Eddie Devlin of Coalisland enjoys a unique distinction in the history of the All-Ireland minor championship by virtue of his involvement in both the 1947 and 1948 Tyrone wins. What is this distinction?

7. Barney Eastwood became a famous boxing promoter, but in 1948 he played a key role for Tyrone minors as a freetaker. How many points did he score in the decider?

8. Which club ground served as the training base for the Tyrone minors during the successful 1947 and 1948 campaigns?

9. Those historic double successes for Tyrone also contributed to a first for Ulster that has, so far, never been repeated. What is that unique achievement?

10. After winning the All-Irelands in 1947 and 1948, Tyrone lost to which county in 1949?

Tyrone's Senior Provincial Breakthrough Years

For many, the glorious breakthrough of the 1956 and 1957 Ulster campaigns remains one of the most important of Tyrone's success. It's still remembered with a great degree of fondness by those who were following the fortunes of the county at the time. Those legendary teams also provided inspiration for a new generation with their history-making exploits.

1. Tyrone played three matches on their way to the 1956 Ulster title. Derry were beaten in the first round and Cavan in the final. Who did Tyrone account for in the semi-final?

2. Jody O'Neill from Coalisland was captain of the team due to the fact that his club had won the county title the previous year. As well as being the first Ulster senior-winning captain, what other distinction did he earn that day in Clones?

3. Three goals proved all important in dethroning the mighty Cavan in the provincial decider. They were scored by players from the Omagh and Dungannon clubs. Can you name them?

4. Just one substitute player was used by Tyrone in the final. Can you name the long-serving player whose introduction at half-time was seen as a reward for years of dedicated service?

5. In the All-Ireland semi-final, Tyrone lost by 0-8 to 0-6 to Galway. What moment early in the second half of that game was seen as ultimately proving the difference between the teams?

6. As well as winning the Anglo Celt Cup, what were the other three competitions won by Tyrone in 1956-57 that helped to make those years so successful?

7. There were a number of changes to the Tyrone line-up in 1957 from the previous historic year. The enforced absence of Iggy Jones due to injury was particularly frustrating. In what unusual location was his injury sustained?

8. Tyrone returned to the Ulster final in 1957, where their opponents were Derry, captained by Jim McKeever. Can you name the captain of the Red Hand county on that occasion and who he replaced as skipper?

9. Injuries to which two influential players were viewed as having a serious negative impact on Tyrone's hopes of winning the All-Ireland semi-final against Louth in 1957?

10. As well as reaching the All-Ireland semi-final for the first time, can you name the other significant Croke Park first achieved by the Tyrone team in that 1956/57 era?

Not so Swinging Sixties

The 1960s was a decade when the glories of 1956 and 1957 seemed to be a distant memory. Almost annual Ulster championship defeats proved demoralising and there was little progress on the youth scene either. But there were glimpses of light, so the swinging sixties are justifiably remembered by some with a certain degree of satisfaction.

1. When Tyrone won the All-Ireland junior title in 1968, the team had two direct connections with the 1956 senior side. One was Frankie Donnelly, who played in the forwards. Who was the other?

2. Which two counties did Tyrone defeat in the All-Ireland junior final and 'Home' final in that 1968 campaign?

3. The Ulster minor league has often provided a launching pad for Tyrone teams in the grade. In what year of the 1960s was this title first won by a team from the county?

4. Jody O'Neill last represented Tyrone in the Ulster senior championship in 1968. Before that, who was the last member of the 1956 and 1957 teams to play in the provincial title-race?

5. Tyrone reached four Ulster minor finals in the 1960s – the years being 1965, 1967, 1968 and 1969. How many times and in which years did they win the title?

6. Can you name the future Ulster GAA president who first represented Tyrone in the Ulster championship in 1962 and for a final time in 1967?

7. Ulster was the dominant force during the golden era of the Railway Cup in the 1960s. Who were the three players from Tyrone who won medals for the province in those years and the two others to play in the final?

8. Many of the Tyrone team which won the Ulster title in 1973 made their Ulster debuts during the 1960s. Barney McAnespie was the second in 1966, but which player and in what year was the first?

9. Tyrone's run of four consecutive Ulster first-round defeats from 1963 to 1966 was the worst until 1990-1993. Their heaviest losses were by 12-point margins. One was to Down in 1965. Against which county and in what year was the other?

10. Two Ulster championship titles were won during the 1960s – the minors against Fermanagh in 1967 and the juniors against Armagh in 1968. Who were the two captains of those teams?

Stars of the Seventies

The 1970s was a time when the distinctive hairstyles and footballing characteristics of the players stood out. There was a certain abandon to their efforts as Tyrone dreamed of Sam Maguire success. That ultimate honour didn't come then, but the seniors, minors and U-21s blazed a trail.

1. How many Ulster titles in total in the minor, U-21 and senior grades did Tyrone teams win in the 1970s?

2. The year 1973 was unique as the first in which Tyrone completed the provincial treble. Four players in that successful season captained their teams to titles. Can you name the quartet?

3. Frank McGuigan will be remembered for many achievements, not least as the youngest Ulster-title-winning Tyrone captain. What other distinction did he achieve in the 1972 Ulster final?

4. One forward on the 1973 Tyrone team led the way in terms of scoring. His tally of 0-17 in the three Ulster championship matches was a record for that year. Who was the player in question?

5. Which Tyrone player represented the county in goal during the 1972 minor campaign and then moved to midfield for the All-Ireland-winning 1973 season?

6. Tyrone's 1973 minors drew with Cork at the penultimate stage of their All-Ireland campaign. They won the replay by 3-10 to 0-10, but what was unique about the hat-trick of goals scored on that occasion?

7. New rules introduced by the GAA mean that Damien O'Hagan's record of playing four years at minor level is unlikely to be equalled in the future. Who is the other Tyrone player to achieve this very notable distinction?

8. In 1976, Paul Donnelly of Augher captained the Tyrone minors to Ulster success. They also led Cork in the All-Ireland semi-final when his involvement in the game ended for what reason?

9. Can you name the five players who started the
   1975 All-Ireland minor final and the 1976 All-Ireland
   semi-final who were also on the first fifteen when
   Tyrone reached their first All-Ireland senior decider
   a decade later?

10. Tyrone's only loss in an Ulster minor final during
    the 1970s came in 1979. One member of that year's
    panel – who missed the final because of a trip to
    the US – went on to gain international acclaim in
    another sporting sphere. Can you name him?

Remembering that First All-Ireland Senior Final

A popular song stated how Tyrone were going to bring the Sam Maguire home. At half-time, the All-Ireland was within reach, and some supporters might even have been contemplating the homecoming celebrations. While Kerry won, and shattered the dream, that 1986 run is still one to recall with pride.

1. Tyrone's run to the Ulster title in 1986 began against Derry in Omagh. Which unlikely player scored the all-important goal in that game?

2. What was unusual about the goal scored by Plunkett Donaghy for Tyrone in the 1986 Ulster final against Down?

3. One of the assistant managers to Art McRory in 1986 was Tom McKeagney. With which club did he make history during the 1970s?

4. Kevin McCabe's penalty goal is widely credited with sealing Tyrone's All-Ireland final place. Which Tyrone player was fouled?

5. In the 1986 Sam Maguire decider, Tyrone manager Art McRory had a family connection with which star Kerry forward?

6. What was the one change in personnel on the Tyrone starting team for the 1986 final against Kerry from the win at the penultimate stage against Galway?

7. The honour of being the first Tyrone player to score in an All-Ireland senior football final fell to which forward in that 1986 team?

8. It was a tale of two penalties in the 1986 final between Tyrone and Kerry. Kevin McCabe's shot went over the bar, but what was the outcome of the Jack O'Shea spot kick right at the start of the game?

9. By how many points were Tyrone ahead after Paudge Quinn scored their goal early in the second half of the 1986 decider?

10. Which three substitutes were introduced by the team manager, Art McRory, during the second half of the final and the three players that they replaced?

Round 23

Making the Sam Maguire Breakthrough

Generations of GAA fans and players from Tyrone dreamed of one day seeing the county win the Sam Maguire Cup. That dream was, of course, finally realised in 2003, so how clearly can you remember the details of what happened on that occasion?

1. How many members of the Tyrone minor team that won the 1998 All-Ireland title went on to start in either the 2003, 2005 or 2008 All-Ireland senior finals?

2. Cormac McAnallen's move to fullback for the replayed Ulster final in 2003 was hailed as a decisive move. But which player did he replace in that position for the game?

3. In the replayed Ulster final victory over Down in 2003, what was the significance of the total number of points scored by Peter Canavan?

4. After the first half of the All-Ireland semi-final against Kerry, how many minutes of additional time were added by the referee?

5. Can you name the two players who started the 2003 All-Ireland final who had not won Ulster or All-Ireland minor medals with the county?

6. Which of the Tyrone players who started that famous game against Armagh was not born in Ireland?

7. Tyrone played eight games during their run to that historic first ever All-Ireland title. Which teams were defeated by them from the Ulster first round onwards?

8. In the 2003 All-Ireland senior final, can you name the Tyrone defender fouled in the incident that resulted in the sending off of Armagh's Diarmuid Marsden?

9. The double-substitution of Peter Canavan in the 2003 All-Ireland final was a particular highlight. Who replaced him in the game and who did he subsequently come back on for?

10. An estimated attendance of how many people welcomed the victorious Tyrone team at their main homecoming event in Omagh on Monday 29 September 2003?

A Glorious Time for Tyrone's Golden Generation

Tyrone GAA fans have been spoiled with magic occasions during the past decade and longer. The All-Ireland successes in 2003, 2005, and 2008 have yielded a whole series of important moments, and saw players become household names within the county and further afield. So, how about looking more closely at the 2005 triumph?

1. Tyrone's ten-game Ulster and All-Ireland campaigns were seen as something of a record. How many draws and against which teams did they have in the 2005 championship?

2. Which two Tyrone players were sent off by the referee, Michael Collins, in the 2005 Ulster final replay against Armagh?

3. Peter Canavan's winning point in the All-Ireland semi-final has been immortalised, but which of his teammates was fouled for the free to be awarded?

4. On the Tyrone team that defeated Kerry in the 2005 All-Ireland final, what were the changes to the starting fifteen players from the starting fifteen in the 2003 All-Ireland final?

5. The goal scored by Tyrone in the 2005 final is a classic. Owen Mulligan delivered the final pass to Peter Canavan after catching a long delivery from which other player?

6. What was the final score in the 2005 final and which of the Tyrone players finished top scorers for them in the game?

7. Who were the three subs introduced by Mickey Harte in the final?

8. How many different clubs were represented on the starting fifteen players in the 2005 All-Ireland final?

9. Following Tyrone's second Sam Maguire Cup success, which two long-serving players announced that they would be retiring from the inter-county scene?

10. Where did the Tyrone manager, Mickey Harte, and team captain, Brian Dooher, first take the Sam Maguire Cup when they crossed the border into the county?

Round

25

A Place in History Secured with the Third Sam

F ew people expected Tyrone to feature in the closing stages of the 2008 All-Ireland, especially after an early Ulster exit. But then they got going through the backdoor and the momentum took them all the way to Croke Park on All-Ireland final day. How good is your memory of that summer campaign?

1. The performance and late scoring exploits of which Tyrone player when introduced as a substitute in the 2008 Ulster first-round replay against Down was especially noteworthy?

2. Sean Cavanagh raised a few eyebrows when he compared Louth's home pitch at Drogheda to which English soccer ground ahead of the All-Ireland qualifiers in 2008?

3. Tyrone defeated Mayo at Croke Park in 2008 to reach the All-Ireland quarter final. How many times have the counties met in senior championship football?

4. Apart from Mayo and Louth, which other county did Tyrone defeat in the All-Ireland qualifiers in 2008?

5. Tyrone scored 3-14 in their All-Ireland quarter-final win over Dublin in 2008. How many of those scores came from play and who scored the three goals?

6. By what margin did the Red Hands defeat Wexford in the 2008 All-Ireland semi-final?

7. What was the rather unusual gesture carried out by many members of the Tyrone team during their progress to the 2008 All-Ireland title?

8. What was the final score when Tyrone defeated Kerry in the 2008 All-Ireland final?

9. Who were the three players whose late points clinched the victory and a third Sam Maguire triumph?

10. Of the team that started the 2008 All-Ireland final, how many of the players had also started the 2003 and 2005 deciders?

Round

26

Scores
and Scorers

Some of the scoring feats produced by star players over the years have been truly amazing. All the big ones are recalled and the totals totted up by them are inevitably popular quiz questions. So, here goes with some of the most significant of all.

1. The performance of Frank McGuigan in the 1984 Ulster final is rightly regarded as one of the greatest ever. Tyrone scored 0-15 that day and he scored 11 of those points. Which players completed the tally?

2. Tyrone's teams have scored four goals in their five All-Ireland senior final appearances. Can you name the players who hit the net for the county during those Sam Maguire deciders?

Leabharlanna Poiblí Chathair Bhaile Átha Cliath
Dublin City Public Libraries

3. Three points in the closing stages of the 2003 All-Ireland final clinched an historic success for Tyrone. Which two players fired over those vital points?

4. In the 1995 All-Ireland final, Peter Canavan scored all but one of Tyrone's 12 points against Dublin. Who got the remaining score?

5. The final score in the 1980 Ulster final between Tyrone and Armagh was among the highest ever. What was it?

6. In 1985, Tyrone reached the National League semi-final at Croke Park. The game against Monaghan ended in a draw thanks to a score from which unlikely source?

7. What is the highest ever total recorded by a Tyrone senior team in the championship at Croke Park?

8. Which player, who came on as a substitute, scored the very last point in the 2008 All-Ireland final win over Kerry?

9. Which two players, ranked as super-subs for much of the campaign, scored the brace of winning goals that clinched the Anglo Celt Cup for Tyrone in the 1995 Ulster final?

10. The point that wasn't in the 1995 All-Ireland final will forever be debated within Tyrone. Peter Canavan got it, but who was the player who gave him the pass?

Notable Tyrone Scoring Records

Tyrone's position as a key challenge at provincial and All-Ireland level for many years has ensured them a high profile and the statistics compiled over those years have also helped to emphasise some of the most notable contributions, which are the subject of this round.

1. When Tyrone met Fermanagh in a Dr Lagan Cup encounter in October 1956, Frankie Donnelly set an individual scoring record. What was it?

2. Frankie Donnelly also topped the Ulster scoring charts for the championship on three occasions. 1956 and 1957 were two, but what was the other?

3. Tyrone's run up to the 1980 Ulster final was particularly high-scoring. Which two players shared the honour of topping the provincial scoring charts that year?

4. Peter Canavan has topped the scoring chart for the Ulster championship on four occasions. In which years he did do so?

5. Which Tyrone players, apart from Frankie Donnelly and Peter Canavan, have emerged as top scorers in the Ulster senior championship?

6. Two Tyrone players have topped the All-Ireland scoring charts. Peter Canavan was the first and the second was Stephen O'Neill in 2005. What was Stephen O'Neill's tally in that season?

7. Which two Tyrone players finished highest in the 2013 All-Ireland scoring charts and what were their totals?

8. Tyrone's 1997 All-Ireland minor semi-final ranks as one of the greatest minor games. How much did Mark Harte score on that occasion at Parnell Park?

9. What is the highest total ever registered by a Tyrone team in an All-Ireland senior, minor or U-21 final?

10. Apart from Peter Canavan, which Tyrone player has scored the most in an All-Ireland senior, minor or U-21 final?

They were Fantastic Captains

Peter Canavan lifted the Sam Maguire for Tyrone after the 2003 All-Ireland final. Other players, too, have enjoyed their own moments in the sun, leading the Red Hands to glorious successes. Who were they, though?

1. Peter Canavan lifted the Sam Maguire Cup for Tyrone in 2003. Before and including that success, to how many inter-county titles did he captain the county?

2. Who was the winning captain of the Tyrone senior team that won the Ulster title in 2001 and what was unusual about the manner of the presentation of the Anglo Celt Cup?

3. Who was the 2001 Tyrone All-Ireland-winning minor captain and what was the unique second honour which he went on to achieve that year?

4. Tyrone have now played in five All-Ireland senior football finals. Can you name the players who captained them in each of those deciders?

5. The 1992 National League decider which Tyrone lost is seen as a missed opportunity. Which player captained them in that final against Derry?

6. Which player from the Cookstown Fr Rocks club has captained Tyrone minor teams to All-Ireland success?

7. Frank McGuigan famously captained Tyrone to the 1973 Ulster title. Who were the captains of the teams that lost the Ulster senior finals of 1972 and 1980?

8. Staying on the theme of losing Ulster finals, can you name the captain of the Tyrone team that missed out against Monaghan in the 1988 provincial decider?

9. Which member of a well-known Tyrone GAA set of brothers captained the county to their third Thomas Markham Cup success in 1973?

10. The late Cormac McAnallen holds a unique record in the annals of the GAA. What is it?

Tyrone Teams Under the Management of Mickey Harte

C urrent Tyrone team manager Mickey Harte
first took charge at inter-county level in 1991.
He has enjoyed an unbroken run at minor, U-21
and senior level since then, but what about the players
who have been part of those teams over more than
two decades?

1. Who was the captain of the first Tyrone minor team
   to reach an Ulster final under the management of
   Mickey Harte?

2. Which two members of the 1993 Tyrone minor
   team went on to play for the county seniors in the
   All-Ireland final a decade later?

3. In all grades and all competitions at minor, U-21 and senior, how many provincial and All-Ireland finals have Tyrone teams appeared in under the management of Mickey Harte?

4. Tyrone have been most successful in the Dr McKenna Cup since the start of 2004. Who captained them to the 2014 title?

5. Which county have Tyrone yet to meet in the Ulster senior championship under the management of Mickey Harte?

6. Since 2003, on how many occasions have Tyrone reached the All-Ireland quarter finals? For a bonus, can you name the teams that they have played each time?

7. In Ulster and All-Ireland championship football since 2003, one county has defeated Tyrone twice as many times as any other. Which county was this?

8. In what year did the current Tyrone assistant manager, Tony Donnelly, first become officially involved in the senior backroom team?

9. Can you name the Tyrone captains in all competitions who have led the county to National League, Dr McKenna Cup and Ulster or All-Ireland senior titles since 2003?

10. What was significant for the team manager about Tyrone's All-Ireland semi-final defeat to Mayo in 2013?

On the All-Ireland Football Stage

There was a time when an appearance at All-Ireland level generated huge levels of excitement and anticipation. Progress to a quarter-final, semi-final or final is still viewed with immense pride and this round focuses on some of Tyrone's achievements on the national stage.

1. How many years was it in 2014 since a Tyrone team first played in an All-Ireland semi-final?

2. Which counties that have been defeated by Tyrone teams in their All-Ireland minor and U-21 final successes?

3. Which three brothers have all represented Tyrone in the same position at All-Ireland level within a decade?

4. What unique record did a Coalisland player set when Tyrone completed the All-Ireland minor and U-21 double in 2001?

5. Three generations of one family have all played for the Red Hand county at All-Ireland minor, U-21 and senior level. Can you name them and the years?

6. The rivalry between Tyrone and Kerry has become especially noteworthy. On how many occasions have Tyrone teams played Kerry in All-Ireland minor, U-21 and senior finals?

7. Which Tyrone player holds the record of having scored most in the county's twenty-four matches in the All-Ireland qualifiers since 2002?

8. The total recorded in the 1991 All-Ireland U-21 final is the highest ever by a Tyrone team. But what was their lowest in a national decider?

9. In the twelve years of the so-called back-door system, can you name the different counties that Tyrone teams have played?

10. For what reason was the first ever All-Ireland quarter-final appearance by a Tyrone senior team particularly frustrating and disappointing?

Historic Facts from a Golden Era

Four decades ago Tyrone scored their third Ulster senior title, and another step towards them becoming one of the top teams in the country was completed. This round focuses on just some of the achievements recorded during a golden spell.

1. Tyrone completed the Ulster treble in 1973 and again in 2001. During the decade 2000-2010, how many times and in what years did they complete the provincial double?

2. Which three players won the RTÉ Man of the Match awards for Tyrone in the 2003, 2005 and 2008 All-Ireland finals?

3. In 2008, Tyrone won the All-Ireland minor and senior double. Prior to that, what counties had won the two titles in the one year?

4. Which current county senior player scored the equalising point for Tyrone in the 2008 All-Ireland minor final against Mayo?

5. How many and who were the Tyrone players who, in 2003, joined a select group who had won All-Ireland minor, U-21 and senior medals during their careers?

6. Can you name the two managers of the Tyrone U-21 team that reached the All-Ireland final in 2003?

7. What was unusual about Tyrone's first-round Ulster championship clash against Derry in 2006?

8. How many Ulster and All-Ireland football titles have been won by Tyrone teams at minor, U-21 and senior levels between 1990 and 2014?

9. Who were the Tyrone team captains for the All-Ireland U-21 and minor successes in the decade from 2000-2010?

10. Prior to 2014, what was the last year that none of the Tyrone minor, U-21 or senior teams progressed to an Ulster semi-final?

Tyrone's National League Fortunes

Each spring, the routine of travelling to far-flung venues enlivens the Red Hand fans from their winter slumber. The National League has provided the bread and butter action for decades and Tyrone have enjoyed some particularly notable achievements.

1. The Dr Lagan Cup was played as a qualifying competition for the National League. How many teams, including Tyrone, competed in the cup?

2. Prior to their first ever final appearance in 1992, in how many National League semi-finals had Tyrone appeared?

3. When Tyrone won the National League Division Two title in 1973, which counties did they defeat in the semi-final and final at Croke Park?

4. Tyrone's new-look team in the 1991-1992 National League defeated the then All-Ireland finalists, Dublin, by how many points at Croke Park in the autumn of 1991?

5. Which novel pairing featured in Tyrone's NFL campaign when the competition was restructured for the 1993-1994 season?

6. Which two counties were defeated by Tyrone in the National League finals of 2002 and 2003?

7. How many minutes of football, excluding added time, did it take to separate Tyrone and Galway when they met in the 2004 National League semi-final?

8. Tyrone reached the National League Division Two final in 2011. But in what year were they relegated to the second tier?

9. Ahead of the 2013 National League final against Dublin, what incident was viewed as having a significant negative impact on Tyrone's chances of winning?

10. Can you name the counties that Tyrone defeated in their 2014 Division One league campaign?

Focusing on the International Series

For better or worse, the International Series played under Compromise Rules have been an annual feature of the GAA calendar year for some time. Tyrone players have featured strongly since the first one in 1984 and more of them than you might think have won caps. So, here goes with a few teasers.

1. Who was the one Tyrone player to be selected on the Ireland team that played the Australians in the first games under Compromise Rules in 1984?

2. John Lynch's one cap for Ireland may well be recalled for his altercation with an Australian opponent, but in what year did the teak-tough defender play for his country?

3. When the Australians returned to Ireland in 1987, one of their games was against Ulster in Omagh. But the game was spoiled by what?

4. Can you name the members of the 1986 Tyrone team who represented Ireland in the International Series?

5. Sean Cavanagh is the leading capped player from Tyrone in the Compromise Rules. Two more are in joint second. Who are they?

6. In what year was the Cormac McAnallen Trophy for the international rules series first presented?

7. The year in which most Tyrone players represented Ireland was 2005, when there were six on the panel. Can you name the Red Hand stars involved?

8. Just hours before travelling to Australia for the 2008 series, what other important sporting event did Sean Cavanagh play in?

9. Apart from Peter Canavan, Sean Cavanagh and Cormac McAnallen, who were the other members of the 2003 All-Ireland-winning Tyrone team to play for Ireland during their careers?

10. A total of nineteen different players from Tyrone have represented Ireland. How many different clubs are included in that list?

Round

34

They were
All Stars

E ach autumn brings with it the sense of anticipation
as the GAA All Stars are nominated and then
announced. Tyrone's All-Ireland titles in the 2000s
have ensured that they are now among the most successful
counties.

1. The Moy club holds the distinction of having the most
   players honoured as All Stars. Can you name them?

2. Tyrone's progress to their first All-Ireland final in
   1986 earned them recognition in that year's All Star
   team. Which players received awards?

3. All Stars trips to various countries have been a feature
   of the scheme since 1971. Which Tyrone man managed
   the All Stars against Kerry during the 1987 trip to San
   Francisco?

4. Bank of Ireland was replaced by Powerscreen as the official sponsors of the All Stars schemes. In what years did Powerscreen sponsor the hurling and football awards?

5. Peter Canavan and Sean Cavanagh are the Tyrone players with the most All Stars. But who is next on the list?

6. Since the All Stars scheme was launched in 1971, can you name the years in which Tyrone won an Ulster title, but then subsequently failed to earn recognition on the All Star team?

7. Tyrone's best ever years in terms of All Star representation were the eight and seven players named in the 2005 and 2008 teams. Can you name the seven recipients on the 2003 team?

8. How many goalkeepers from the O'Neill county have earned places on the football All Stars?

9. Eugene McKenna won three All Star awards in the Ulster title-winning years of 1984, 1986 and 1989. What was the other notable aspect of his trio of accolades?

10. And, finally to the county's first ever All Star winner. Who was he, in what year did he win his award and what position did he earn on the team?

And Finally ... Special Honours on Tyrone's Playing Fields

History-making records inevitably provoke much discussion and some are truly remarkable. To finish, then, here is a look at some of the players whose individual honours and length of service mean that they stand out above all others.

1. An open draw championship was organised to mark the GAA Centenary Year in 1984. What was unique about the trophy presented for the winners of that competition in Tyrone?

2. When Tyrone reached the 1980 Ulster final, Damien O'Hagan was playing a starring role for what club?

3. What age was given for Ardboe's Patsy Forbes when he played his last county final for the club against Trillick in 1983?

4. Who is the oldest player known to have won a senior championship medal?

5. A total of three players have captained their clubs to three O'Neill Cup titles? Can you name the historic trio?

6. The trophy for the winners of Division One of the All-County League is presented in memory of which former Tyrone footballer?

7. In 1977 three brothers all represented Tyrone at senior inter-county level. Who were they?

8. Which Moy player represented Tyrone at senior level before going on to play for Tipperary?

9. Which member of the 1973 Tyrone team went on to play against his native county in the Ulster championship?

10. Three of the McConnell brothers have scored goals for Tyrone at minor, U-21 and senior level. What other notable achievement do Finbar, Brian and Pascal hold?

Founder Members Make Their Mark

1. Michael V. O'Nolan's son, Brian, wrote under the name Myles n gCopaleen/Flann O'Brien.
2. It was unfinished due to darkness.
3. Work in the bogs around the area.
4. The McAnespie Cup.
5. Eoin O'Duffy.
6. They failed to score against Armagh, the game finishing 2-1 to 0-0.
7. Blue.
8. The Rose Kavanagh camogie club.
9. In 1927, Tyrone played Kildare, who had just been crowned All-Ireland champions.
10. It included the first penalty to be taken in a Gaelic football game.

1. John Houston Stewart was vice-president of the GAA in 1885. Dr Hugh Alexander Auchinleck made an important contribution to the formulation of the Rules of Hurling in 1883.
2. 'Mountains of Pomeroy'.
3. Dr Patrick McCartan, a native of Carrickmore.
4. George McGuigan. He stood for the presidency in the year that Paddy MacFlynn was elected.
5. Frank O'Neill from Coalisland, Peter Harte from Ballygawley and Brian McLernon from Derrylaughan.
6. James Treacy.
7. Des McMahon.
8. Joseph Martin served as chief executive of the Western Education and Library Board.
9. He was 34.
10. Paddy Cullen and Paul Doris.

Who am I?

1. Paddy Donnelly (Trillick).
2. Ned Magee.
3. Charles Curran.
4. John McGuckian, representing Ballinderry on that Tyrone minor team.
5. Seamus Campbell from Coalisland.
6. Brian Cullen (Dungannon).
7. Seamus Bonner (Omagh).
8. Eddie Devlin, who was 15 at the time of that Hogan Cup final.
9. Paddy O'Neill, who served as Tyrone County Secretary 1952-1976.
10. John Begley, Carrickmore, uncle of Brian McEniff.

<table>
<tr><td>Round</td><td rowspan="2"># Men on the Line who Made the Decisions</td></tr>
<tr><td>4</td></tr>
</table>

Men on the Line who Made the Decisions

Round 4

1. Gerry Brown.
2. 1976.
3. Donal Donnelly and Art McRory.
4. Jody O'Neill.
5. 1976.
6. Frank Martin.
7. Four (1991, 1993, 1997 and 1998).
8. Raymond Munroe (Carrickmore).
9. Fr Gerard McAleer (Beragh) and Paddy Tally (Galbally).
10. John Donnelly (Trillick).

Top Aces in Handball

1. M.J. Kelly.
2. Moy.
3. U-14 in 1986.
4. Mickey Kerr (Beragh), who was a corner forward on the 1956 Tyrone team.
5. Drumquin.
6. The venue for the game was switched due to a slippery alley.
7. Johnny Woods (Brackey).
8. John Curran (Loughmacrory).
9. 1867.
10. New covered one-wall handball alleys.

With the Referees

1. A native of Armagh, he refereed the 1972 All-Ireland final replay and the 1974 final.
2. The Whistler's Inn.
3. MacRory Cup final.
4. Gerry McCabe (Clonoe).
5. Patsy Lynn (Toome) Antrim, 1977.
6. The referee, Eamon McHugh (Aghyaran) was unable to continue due to injury and was replaced by Eugene McConnell (Clogher).
7. They played Kerry in the final and, Michael Collins, the referee, was from Cork.
8. He refereed three All-Ireland finals in the 1960s – minor in 1963 and U-21 in 1965 and 1966.
9. John Devlin performed as linesman at a Leinster senior hurling final in 1992.
10. Jim Curran refereed the 1993 All-Ireland Club final and the Ulster senior final in 1992.

Which Club am I?

1. Owen Roes. The team was based in the Leckpatrick area.
2. Killyclogher St Mary's.
3. Moortown St Malachy's.
4. Carrickmore Éire Ógs.
5. Fintona Pearses.
6. Galbally Pearses.
7. Killyman St Mary's.
8. Dromore St Dympna's.
9. Brackaville Owen Roes.
10. Carrickmore St Colmcille's.

Hurlers on the Ditch

1. He finished top scorer in the league.
2. He won the All-Ireland Poc Fada title.
3. Ciaran McBride won All-Ireland underage titles with Tyrone hurlers.
4. Terry McCann (Killyclogher).
5. Donegal, Fermanagh and Fingal.
6. Six. Minors in 1986 and 1987, seniors in 2009, 2011, 2013 and 2014.
7. Damien Casey (Dungannon).
8. Play for Ulster in an inter-provincial final.
9. Tom McGill (Derry).
10. Armagh in 2010.

Camogie to the Fore

1. She also refereed an All-Ireland final.
2. 44.
3. The 1980 All-Ireland junior final.
4. Edendork (1976), Ardboe (1999), and Clonoe 2000 and 2002).
5. They each played for Ulster.
6. Pat Darcy.
7. Carrickmore and Dungannon.
8. 1990 and 1991.
9. Shauna Jordan
10. Carrickmore and Eglish.

The New Kids on the Block from Ladies Football

1. It was the penultimate occasion in which a cup was presented in the old Hogan Stand. The cup was presented to Nuala McCartan (Beragh).
2. Sinead McLaughlin (Drumragh) was captain. Niall Colton and Colm Donnelly from Dromore were the managers.
3. Eilis Gormley and Lynette Hughes (Carrickmore), Lynda Donnelly (St Macartan's) and Claire McGarvey (Errigal Ciaran).
4. The Masterskreen Trophy.
5. She scored 3-6.
6. Four – 2000, 2001, 2008 and 2012.
7. Errigal Ciaran.
8. 2011.
9. Four, last won by Tyrone in 2009.
10. She was the first Tyrone player to captain Ulster to the inter-provincial title.

Round 11

School Days were the Best of our Lives

1. Mick Brewster, after whom Brewster Park in Enniskillen is named.
2. Eugene Mulligan (Cookstown).
3. He captained the team.
4. Colm McAleer.
5. Kevin O'Brien (Dromore) and Paul McGurk (Cookstown).
6. They shared the title with St Michael's Enniskillen after the final was postponed due to an outbreak of Foot and Mouth disease.
7. Tim Harney (with Armagh) and Ronan McNabb and Peter Hughes (with Tyrone).
8. The final between Omagh CBS and St Patrick's Academy, Dungannon, was the first all-Tyrone decider.
9. 1967 and 2008.
10. 2008.

County Senior Finals

1. Dromore (1977 and 1978), Fintona (1979).
2. It came after they had lost the three previous finals.
3. Five finals (1946, 1977, 1978, 1992, 2004).
4. The game against Omagh did not take place.
5. They played eight finals: 1994, 1996 (replay), 2000 (replay), 2001 and 2006 (replay).
6. Seven – Errigal Ciaran, Carrickmore, Killyclogher, Omagh, Dromore, Clonoe, Coalisland.
7. That final had seven goals, which is the most ever scored in a Tyrone senior decider.
8. Three – Omagh, Clonoe and Carrickmore.
9. Nine in total.
10. The hundredth final will take place in 2016.

Do you Remember that County Final?

1. 1998 in Pomeroy.
2. The game was broadcast via a telephone in a nearby house.
3. They were all played in December.
4. Derrylaughan, Ardboe, Eglish and Augher.
5. 1996. Carrickmore took the lead on the Roll of Honour when they won their eleventh title.
6. Owen Roes and Gortin.
7. 17 points. The final score was 3-9 to 0-1.
8. 1981.
9. Cookstown lost to Fintona by 0-3 to 0-0 in 1938.
10. Last drawn final up to 2014 was in 2006 – Carrickmore v Errigal Ciaran.

Testing Your Memory on this Century's O'Neill's Cup Deciders

1. Two – the 2000 and 2006 finals.
2. All the previous winning captains.
3. Peter McGinnity and Brian Meenan.
4. Errigal Ciaran (2000, 2006 and 2012), Carrickmore (2001), Killyclogher (2003), Clonoe (2008 and 2013).
5. Raymond Munroe (2000), Mickey Harte (2002), Seamus Goodwin (2009), Damien O'Hagan and Peter Heron (2010).
6. Dermot Carlin (Killyclogher) in 2003 and Conor Gormley (Carrickmore) in 2005.
7. Six (2000, 2001, 2004, 2005, 2006 and 2013).
8. He was captain and he scored winning goals from a late penalty.
9. They played semi-final, semi-final replay and final all in the space of eight days.
10. Dromore and Errigal Ciaran with three titles each.

1. Downpatrick and Enniskillen Gaels.
2. Ardboe (1972), Trillick (1974), Coalisland (1989) and Omagh (2014).
3. Carrickmore, Ardboe and Trillick.
4. 1977.
5. Three. After defeating Crossmaglen, they went on to defeat Enniskillen Gaels in the final.
6. St Gall's and Derrygonnelly.
7. The match between Ardboe and Clann Na nGael of Lurgan was abandoned and both teams disqualified after a row broke out.
8. Errigal Ciaran manager, Ronan McGuckin, was a native of Ballinderry.
9. St Eunan's, Letterkenny and Ballinderry.
10. Errigal Ciaran in 1995.

Round 16 — The Ulster Junior and Intermediate Scenes

1. 2004.
2. Trillick 2008 and Cookstown 2009 and 2012.
3. Stewartstown (2004), Greencastle (2006), Rock (2007), Derrytresk (2011).
4. Both finals featured teams from Tyrone – Stewartstown and Pomeroy.
5. Martin Conway and Sean Teague.
6. Rock (2008) and Derrytresk (2012).
7. Naomh Colmcille in 2010.
8. Fergal Logan, Ciaran Gourley and Owen Mulligan.
9. Brackaville and Killeeshil at junior level and Eskra at Intermediate. Dungannon lost the Intermediate final in 2001 when competition was unofficial.
10. He is the Tyrone player who has won most titles at Croke Park.

1. Separate leagues for teams from east and west Tyrone.
2. 1979.
3. It was their first since 2000.
4. Six.
5. First.
6. Six (2003, 2004, 2006, 2007, 2008, 2011).
7. A four division structure with Division 1A and 1B, Division Two and Three.
8. Two, Errigal Ciaran (2002) and Dromore (2007).
9. Five (1995, 1996, 1999, 2002 and 2005).
10. Loughmacrory, Newtownstewart and Killeeshil to Division Two, Eskra, Strabane and Moortown to Division One.

Those History-Making Tyrone Minors

1. Drumcondra.
2. Tom Sullivan (Coalisland).
3. Mick Loftus.
4. Peter O'Reilly from Dublin.
5. Eddie Devlin, Harry Hartop, Sean McGrath, Malachy Dargan and John Joe O'Hagan.
6. He is the only player to captain an All-Ireland minor-football winning team twice.
7. Four.
8. Pomeroy.
9. It is the only time that two Ulster teams have completed the Thomas Markham and Sam Maguire double in successive years. The teams were Tyrone and Cavan.
10. Donegal.

Tyrone's Senior Provincial Breakthrough Years

1. Monaghan on a score of 2-9 to 0-7.
2. He was still a teenager when he captained the side to provincial glory.
3. Jackie Taggart and Donal Donnelly (Omagh) and Iggy Jones (Dungannon).
4. Hugh Kelly (Urney).
5. A save by Jack Mangan of an Iggy Jones shot for goal.
6. Dr Lagan Cup, Dr McKenna Cup and the *Gaelic Weekly* Tournament.
7. He got injured in the Polo Grounds, New York, during Tyrone's US trip.
8. Eddie Devlin (Coalisland), who replaced Iggy Jones.
9. Donal Donnelly and Jody O'Neill.
10. They were the first Tyrone senior team to play at the venue.

1. Jody O'Neill, who managed the team.
2. Mayo and London.
3. 1960.
4. Frankie Donnelly in 1965.
5. Once, in 1967.
6. Peter Harte.
7. Frankie Donnelly, Jody O'Neill and Thady Turbett won medals for Ulster. The two others who played in the finals were Seamus Taggart and Mick Donaghy.
8. Peter Mulgrew in 1965.
9. Antrim in 1963, when Tyrone lost by 2-9 to 0-3.
10. Seamus Donaghy (Dromore) captained the minors and Pat O'Neill (Derrylaughan) captained the juniors.

1. Nine – two U-21, one senior and six minor making a total of nine.
2. Peter Mulgrew (National League Division Two), Frank McGuigan (Ulster senior), Dessie McKenna (Ulster and All-Ireland minor) and Michael Hughes (U-21).
3. He was introduced as a sub in the senior game after winning the minor title with Tyrone.
4. Patsy Hetherington (Donaghmore).
5. Patsy Kerlin (Owen Roes and subsequently Aughabrack and Omagh).
6. All three were scored by the McKenna brothers. Eugene got two and Dessie one.
7. Eddie Devlin played for Tyrone minors in 1946, 1947, 1948 and 1949.
8. He sustained a broken leg.
9. Aidan Skelton, Ciaran McGarvey, Kevin McCabe, Damien O'Hagan and Paddy Ball.
10. Tommy Corr from Clonoe in boxing.

Remembering that First All-Ireland Senior Final

1. Centre half-back, Noel McGinn.
2. A high ball in was caught by the Down goalkeeper who was adjudged to have crossed the line.
3. Augher when they won the Tyrone senior title for the first time.
4. Eugene McKenna.
5. Art McRory's sister-in-law, Marie, was a sister of Kerry attacker Mickey Sheehy.
6. Paddy Ball was introduced for Pat McKeown.
7. Mickey Mallon.
8. It hit the crossbar.
9. Six, on a score of 1-7 to 0-4.
10. The three players introduced were Stephen Conway, Stephen Rice and Aidan O'Hagan, who replaced John Lynch, Eugene McKenna and Mickey Mallon respectively.

1. Eight in 2003 and 2005 and four in 2008.
2. Chris Lawn.
3. His 11 points, matched Frank McGuigan 1984 score.
4. Eight.
5. Conor Gormley and Ryan McMenamin.
6. Ryan McMenamin, born in Toronto.
7. Derry, Antrim, Down, Fermanagh, Kerry and Armagh.
8. Philip Jordan.
9. Brian McGuigan and Gerard Cavlan.
10. 30-40,000.

A Glorious Time for Tyrone's Golden Generation

1. Three, against Cavan, Armagh and Dublin.
2. Stephen O'Neill and Peter Canavan.
3. Stephen O'Neill.
4. Pascal McConnell, Joe McMahon, Michael Magee, Davy Harte, Ryan Mellon and Stephen O'Neill all came into the team.
5. Philip Jordan.
6. The final score was Tyrone 1-16 Kerry 2-10 and the top scorers were Peter Canavan (1-1), Owen Mulligan (0-4) and Stephen O'Neill (0-4).
7. Colin Holmes, Chris Lawn and Peter Canavan.
8. 10.
9. Peter Canavan and Chris Lawn.
10. The grave of Cormac McAnallen.

A Place in History Secured with the Third Sam

1. Tommy McGuigan.
2. Accrington Stanley.
3. Four times – 1989, 2004, 2008 and 2013.
4. Westmeath.
5. 3-13 from play and the goals were scored by Sean Cavanagh, Davy Harte and Joe McMahon.
6. 6 points, 0-23 to 1-14.
7. They grew beards.
8. 1-16 to 2-10.
9. Enda McGinley, Kevin Hughes and Colm Cavanagh.
10. Six – Conor Gormley, Philip Jordan, Ryan McMenamin, Enda McGinley, Brian Dooher and Sean Cavanagh.

Scores and Scorers

1. Eugene McKenna, Noel McGinn, Patsy Kerlin and Colm Donaghy.
2. Paudge Quinn (1986), Peter Canavan (2005) and Tommy McGuigan (2008).
3. Owen Mulligan from a free and Stephen O'Neill (0-2).
4. Jody Gormley (Trillick).
5. 4-10 to 4-7 for Armagh.
6. Ciaran McGarvey, who was full-back in the game.
7. 1-21 in the 2003 All-Ireland quarter-final against Fermanagh.
8. Colm Cavanagh.
9. Adrian Cush and Matt McGleenan.
10. Sean McLaughlin (Drumquin).

Notable Tyrone Scoring Records

1. The total is 23 points. Some accounts have it as 5-8, while others 4-11.

2. 1962.

3. Patsy Hetherington and Patsy Kerlin.

4. 1994, 1995, 1996 and 2003.

5. Patsy Hetherington (1973), Patsy Hetherington and Patsy Kerlin (1980), Frank McGuigan (1984), Stephen Conway (1988), Stephen O'Neill (2005).

6. 5-49 (64 points).

7. Sean Cavanagh (0-29) and Darren McCurry (0-28).

8. 0-12.

9. 4-16 by the U-21s in the 1991 All-Ireland final against Kerry.

10. Eamon McCaffrey (2-2) in the 1991 All-Ireland U-21 final.

They were Fantastic Captains

1. A total of 11 at vocational, minor, U-21 and senior level.
2. Sean Teague received the cup with his arm in a sling.
3. Peter Donnelly. He became first Tyrone player to win All-Ireland minor and U-21 medals in one year.
4. Eugene McKenna (1986), Ciaran Corr (1995), Peter Canavan (2003), Brian Dooher (2005 and 2008).
5. Enda Kilpatrick.
6. Shea McGarrity (2010).
7. Peter Mulgrew (1972) and Kevin McCabe (1980).
8. Plunkett Donaghy.
9. Dessie McKenna (Augher).
10. He is only the second player to have captained All-Ireland-winning minor and U-21 teams. Tommy Diamond of Derry was the first in 1965 and 1968.

1. T.P. Sheehy (Cookstown).
2. Gerard Cavlan and Brian Dooher.
3. A total of seventeen, including six minor, four U-21 and seven senior, excluding the 2005 Ulster replay.
4. Sean Cavanagh.
5. Fermanagh.
6. Nine times. Fermanagh (2003), Mayo (2004), Dublin (2005), Meath (2007), Dublin (2008), Kildare (2009), Dublin (2010), Dublin (2011) and Monaghan (2013).
7. Donegal (four times in 2004, 2011, 2012 and 2013).
8. 2004.
9. NFL – Peter Canavan, All-Ireland – Peter Canavan and Brian Dooher, Ulster – Peter Canavan and Brian Dooher.
10. It was the 200th competitive match in charge of Tyrone for Mickey Harte.

On the All-Ireland Football Stage

1. Eighty three years, since the minors in 1931.
2. Mayo (1948, 2001 and 2008), Dublin (1947 and 2001), Kildare (1973), Galway (1992), Laois (1998), Limerick (2000), Cork (2010), Kerry (1991, 2004, 2005 and 2008).
3. The McConnell brothers from Newtownstewart all played in goal between 1989 and 1998.
4. Peter Donnelly appeared in both.
5. The O'Hagans – John Joe (minor 1947 and 1948, senior 1956 and 1957), Damien (minor 1975, 1976 and 1978 and senior 1984, 1986 and 1989) and Tiarnan (minor 2008).
6. Six – three senior, two minor and one U-21.
7. Sean Cavanagh.
8. 0-4 in the 1975 All-Ireland minor final.
9. Wexford, Leitrim, Derry, Sligo, Down, Galway, Laois, Monaghan, Westmeath, Mayo, Longford, Roscommon, Offaly, Kildare, Meath and Armagh.
10. They lost to Derry in the 2001 quarter-final, having previously defeated them in the championship.

Historic Facts from a Golden Era

1. Four times, in 2001, 2003, 2007 and 2010.
2. Kevin Hughes (2003), Stephen O'Neill (2005), Sean Cavanagh (2008).
3. Kerry and Dublin.
4. Matthew Donnelly.
5. Twelve – Pascal McConnell, Michael McGee, Gavin Devlin, Philip Jordan, Peter Donnelly, Cormac McAnallen, Ryan Mellon, Brian McGuigan, Stephen O'Neill, Enda McGinley, Kevin Hughes and Owen Mulligan.
6. Terry McCann and Peter Doherty.
7. Tyrone failed to score in the first half.
8. Thirty-six in total. Nine Ulster minor, five All-Ireland minor, eight Ulster U-21 and four All-Irelands, seven Ulster senior and three All-Irelands.
9. U-21 Cormac McAnallen (2000 and 2001), minor – Peter Donnelly (2001), Marc Cunningham (2004), Ronan McNabb (2008) and Shea McGarrity (2010).
10. 1983.

Tyrone's National League Fortunes

1. Five.
2. Four – 1957, 1974, 1975 and 1985.
3. Down and Wicklow.
4. 12, 4-11 to 0-11.
5. Kilkenny and Wicklow.
6. Cavan and Laois.
7. 200.
8. 2010.
9. An injury to Stephen O'Neill when he tripped on a ball.
10. Kildare, Westmeath and Mayo.

1. Plunkett Donaghy.
2. 1987.
3. Torrential rain, which resulted in a waterlogged pitch and flooded parts of the town.
4. Plunkett Donaghy, Damien O'Hagan and John Lynch.
5. Peter Canavan and Cormac McAnallen on six each.
6. 2005.
7. Sean Cavanagh, Brian Dooher, Brian McGuigan, Ryan McMenamin, Owen Mulligan, and Stephen O'Neill.
8. The Tyrone intermediate final against Trillick, which Trillick won.
9. Brian Dooher, Brian McGuigan, Ryan McMenamin, Owen Mulligan, Stephen O'Neill, Gerard Cavlan, Colin Holmes, Philip Jordan, Kevin Hughes, Enda McGinley and Brian McGuigan.
10. Thirteen.

1. Plunkett Donaghy, Sean Cavanagh and Philip Jordan.
2. John Lynch, Eugene McKenna, Damien O'Hagan and Plunkett Donaghy.
3. Tony McKenna, who carried out the role as Tyrone County chairman.
4. 1995-1997.
5. Eugene McKenna, Philip Jordan and Conor Gormley (three each).
6. 1973 and 2007.
7. Cormac McAnallen, Conor Gormley, Philip Jordan, Sean Cavanagh, Brian Dooher, Brian McGuigan and Peter Canavan.
8. One, Finbar McConnell in 1996.
9. They came in three different positions – midfield, centre half forward and full-forward.
10. Kevin McCabe in 1980 in the half-back position.

And Finally ... Special Honours on Tyrone's Playing Fields

1. It was a specially commissioned piece of Tyrone crystal.
2. Fermoy in Cork.
3. 43.
4. Mickey Harte (Errigal Ciaran), aged 40.
5. The Jim Devlin Cup, the Frank O'Neill Cup and the Joe McGarrity Cup.
6. Brendan Dolan.
7. Tom, Sean and Brendan Donnelly.
8. John Owens.
9. Liam Turbett.
10. They each hold Ulster medals at minor, U-21 or senior.

Visit our website and discover thousands of other History Press books.

www.thehistorypress.ie

The History Press Ireland